Spirit Tokens
of the
Ling Qi Jing

Ivan Kashiwa

WEATHERHILL
New York • Tokyo

First edition, 1997

Published by Weatherhill, Inc., 568 Broadway, Suite 705, New York, NY 10012. Protected by copyright under the terms of the International Copyright Union; all rights reserved. Except for fair use in book reviews, no part of this book may be reproduced for any reason by any means, including any method of photographic reproduction, without permission of the publisher.

Printed in the United States of America.

Library of Congress Cataloging-in-Publication Data

Tung-fang, Shuo, 154–93 B.C.
    [Ling ch'i ching. English]
    Spirit tokens of the Ling qi jing / [translated, with commentary by] Ivan Kashiwa. — 1st ed.
       p.   cm.
    ISBN 0-8348-0400-X
    1. Divination—China. 2. Fortune-telling—China.
    I. Kashiwa, Ivan. II. Title.
    BF1770.C5T8613 1997
    133.3′3—dc21   97-27680
                                                    CIP

靈樞經

Spirit Tokens
of the
Ling Qi Jing

To Ron Richards and Rob Cook,
fellow seekers

CONTENTS

HOW TO BE A SAGE

How many times have you wondered at the little slips of paper that you find tucked into the folds of the fortune cookie you are given at the end of a meal in a Chinese restaurant? No, they aren't really Chinese at all. In fact, they are unknown in China (though I suspect they will catch on, once someone realizes there's profit in it). But the more "authentic" kind, the kind produced in the fortune cookie factories of San Francisco, Los Angeles, Chicago, and New York, do contain oriental wisdom of a sort. They are based on a long tradition of fortune-telling slips that hang on the walls of temples in China and which began, records show, more than a thousand years ago. You can still find such fortune slips in the temples of Japan, Taiwan, Hong Kong, and Singapore, though they are currently illegal in the Peoples' Republic of China.

These fortune slips are more likely to contain some kind of handy homily ("The wise person, when given a corner can deduce the square") than a true prognostication of the "you will meet a tall dark stranger" type. One slip I picked up in Taiwan almost twenty years ago said: "Recall where you came from—good intentions deserve good responses. Respect your parents as they age. Why act so quickly on the basis of your own emotions?" Since I was considering a relationship at the time—one that both sets of parents opposed—this was good advice, but certainly not my "fortune," whatever I decided to do. As one wag put it, "These aren't fortune cookies, they're 'aphorism cookies.'" What is going on here?

In fact, the ancient Chinese did not believe one's future can be divined with precision any more than most Westerners do. Individuals simply differ too much, and the possible permutations of events in the course of even a single day in each life are simply too great. Ancient Chinese thinkers, living in one of the world's earliest population centers, certainly understood this. There is no high road to the future.

Despite what you may have been led to believe, there is no word in Chinese that exactly corresponds to the English word "fate." One of the Chinese words normally translated "fate," *yun*, refers to the cycles of life through which each individual passes. It is one's response to these cycles that leads to the ups and downs we see in individual lives. Instead of three mysterious sisters spinning the thread of life atop Mt. Olympus, Chinese myth tells of scores of patient celestial bureaucrats recording each person's thoughts and actions in their Book of Life, constantly making additions and deletions. Western foretelling is thus replaced in China by the function of the historian. The notion that an individual is somehow a pawn in the hands of some Great Unseen is simply alien to Chinese ways of thinking.

As the myth of the Books of Life makes clear, Chinese thinkers did not hold that what happens to us is the result of pure luck. Another Chinese word usually translated "fate," *ming*, really means something like "life decree"—it is the ordained future resulting from both the person's current position in the scheme of things and from that person's response to his or her particular circumstances. In this view, our "fate" is constantly changing and we have much to say about its direction. The book you hold in your hands is, true to the culture that produced it, a book of fortune telling that does not admit either predestination or blind chance.

The most widely-known book of Chinese "fortune telling," the *Yijing*, despite its press in the West, has for centuries been regarded in China not as a book of divination, but as a book of wisdom. And what is wisdom? It is the ability to deduce the whole square from a single corner. As one of the oldest commentaries to the *Yijing* has it, "The sage sees the subtle traces left by events as they begin to unfold, and acts accordingly." That would be grand advice if all of us were sages! But at what precise point should Napoleon have known that Waterloo was imminent?

The answer is as simple as it is mysterious. And it has nothing to do with fate and everything to do with the destiny we choose for ourselves. We begin with the obvious. Each event in our lives may be seen to have a beginning, a middle, and end. An event, whether good or bad, fortunate or unfortunate, begins with subtle stirrings like the beginnings of a breeze on the tips of a feather. Then it gains momentum and we are tossed about like fallen leaves. This is the "fate" that thinkers in the West have focused on. By this time we are truly fated to follow the inevitable unfolding of the event. It is too late to do anything except "go with the flow."

Once the event has begun, we take control again. If we are wise in the conventional sense, we gauge how far we have blown and try to change our thinking to account for the distance we have travelled. In short, we either trust blindly in the natural processes we have come to call "fate" or we deceive ourselves into thinking that we are masters of our own destiny after the fact—like my three-year-old, who declares proudly when he falls from his tricycle, "I meant to do that." This is not wisdom. It is self-deception.

The truly wise begin by holding up a feather to catch the event before it even properly begins to be an event. They catch the unfolding. They deliberate and consider. They prepare and plan. When that whisper of a breeze becomes a gale-force wind, they find themselves firmly anchored, or, if the wind is favorable, they already have their sails spread.

This is not something that one does by instinct. Though a few, the "sagely ones," just seem to have a knack, even in their case it is something learned, hopefully not as the result of being blown about too much. Most of us learn slowly. We need a guide. For the past twenty years, ever since I discovered the *Ling Qi Jing* among a cache of ancient texts that had been retrieved from a sand-covered temple in Central Asia, it has served as my guide.

But surely no one seriously believes that a book written down some two thousand years ago could guide our actions in the modern world! Certainly the *Ling Qi Jing* has never advised me not to take an airplane ride. So here's how the ancient Chinese believed the process to work—how the daily process does in fact work, whether you choose to use the *Ling Qi Jing* as your guide or not.

We have established that forthcoming events, whether good, bad or indifferent, cast their shadows into the eternal Now. The problem is that every event, even the most inconsequential, broadcasts its subtle signals. With all that's going on in the world, it's no wonder we are unable to "read" the future and have to concentrate just to ignore the static. It's like tuning in thousands of radio news networks at once. No one can process all that information.

To tune in just those signals that have meaning to you—those which presage the events that will affect your life—you need to concentrate. Paradoxically, nothing concentrates the mind so much as creating a new "event," a mini-event that will cast its own ripples out to interact with the waves of signals around you. Those that reflect your mini-event are the signals of events of importance to you, events with which you are on a collision course. It's a little like radar.

Okay, so it sounds obscure, but it's really something we do every day. Say that you meet a friend and want to find out her mood and gauge her receptivity to a certain proposal you wish to make. You normally begin by saying something entirely inconsequential, like "How's the world treating you today?" The answer, too, is likely to be entirely inconsequential, in informational terms—or is it? In fact, it is the whisper of the upcoming breeze (your friend's mood, her attitude toward you, her willingness to engage with you now, etc.) and you judge it very carefully before proceeding. What you have done is create a "mini-event" to clarify the future. Further, you have, without thinking, allowed that event to focus your concentration on the response your question is likely to elicit at this time. You are now totally concentrating on your friend and "telling your fortune" with regard to her. (It *is* very much like radar, isn't it?)

We regularly employ the same sort of process with respect to the material world around us. Who would venture out onto spring ice without first taking a tentative push with the foot at the ice along the shore to see how much weight it will bear?

This, then, is where the *Ling Qi Jing* comes in. Casting the twelve tokens and reading with care the verse they indicate creates precisely the sort of "mini-event" you need to focus your full attention on the subtle forces at work around you. The "response" might at first seem obscure—it might even seem completely unrelated to the question— but as you meditate on the matter, you will in fact begin to see everything more clearly. You will begin to know what is to come and, more importantly, what you should do about it. In this, the real fortune telling process, the *Ling Qi Jing* excels. As Zhang Shi, writing circa 1178, put it:

> In general, whenever you use the *Ling Qi Jing* to foretell the future, you should analyze all of the motivating forces surrounding the question you have asked. It is not like those other fortune-telling books which broadly indicate that something is "auspicious" or "inauspicious"…Those books are hard to understand and really leave you unsure as to what you should do. The words of the *Ling Qi Jing* are on the contrary simple, but they lead you to deeply contemplate and finally understand.

CONSULTING THE SPIRIT TOKENS

THE TOKENS: You will need twelve disk-shaped tokens, divided into three groups of four. Ancient instructions state that the tokens should be the size of the tokens used for the game of *weiqi* (Japanese *go*) and made from the wood of a tree struck by lightning. But all that is really necessary is that your tokens may be marked with a head and tail, fit easily into your hand, and not be used for any other purpose. Coins in three denominations—say quarters, dimes, and pennies—are ideal. You may also use checkers, marking one set of four to distinguish it from the other of a similar color, or cut your own tokens from a one-inch diameter dowel. My own set is made from flat stones of three different shades that my wife, children, and I found on the beach.

THE TRIGRAMS: The traditional markings on the tokens are are as follows:

上 *shang* ["upper"] on the first four.

中 *zhong* ["central"] on the second four.

下 *xia* ["lower"] on the final four.

If you make your own tokens, the four tokens in each set should be inscribed on one side with the appropriate symbol. If you use coins, let quarters be upper, dimes be central, and pennies be lower. The number of heads you throw in each of the above three groups will form a trigram.

The concept of the trigram comes from the *Yijing*, but it is more fully developed in the *Ling Qi Jing*. The upper number represents heaven, the lower earth, and the middle humanity. All existence is formed of the interplay of heavenly yang and earthly yin forces, yang being the stimulant, aggressive, bright and volatile mode, yin the responsive, receptive, dark, and fecund mode. All human beings, and the world in which they exist, are composed of harmonious (hopefully!) admixtures of both. Yin and yang are not static, but constantly changing into one another.

The *Ling Qi Jing* takes account of this by designating the numbers 1 and 2 as lesser yang and yin, respectively; the numbers 3 and 4 as greater yang and yin. Lesser yang and yin develop into greater and from there into their opposite. Zero is the perfect merging of yin and yang at those nodes where one develops into the other. It thus represents those aspects of a situation that may unfold in unpredictable ways. The developmental cycle can thus be expressed with numbers as follows: 1 > 3 > 0 > 2 > 4 > 0 > 1, and so on.

In the *Ling Qi Jing,* the focus is entirely on you, the representative of humanity, as you cast the stones to aid you in achieving harmony in your space between heaven and earth. As a result, while you will cast a trigram, as in the *Yijing,* there is not here a separate verse for each line. Instead, your attention will be directed by means of a single verse that represents the relationship between the upper, middle, and lower parts of the trigram.

CASTING THE TOKENS: When you wish to direct your mind to a question or event, create a calm space around you. As you hold the twelve tokens in your hands, meditate for a moment on the question you wish to ask and its possible implications. Then, simply allow the tokens to slip from your hands to the table as if they were sand. Next, arrange the tokens in a square, with the four *shang* tokens on top, *zhong* in the middle, and the *xia* tokens on the bottom, taking care to arrange those that have come up heads on the left, as follows:

shang tokens:	● ● ○ ○
zhong tokens:	● ○ ○ ○
xia tokens:	● ○ ○ ○

To locate the appropriate verse in this book, count the number of tokens in each row with the heads—or characters—showing. For example, if two tokens are "face up" in the upper row, the first number of your trigram will be 2. If no heads are showing in that row, the first number will be 0, and so on. Once the three-digit number is determined, turn to that number in the book to begin determining the response to your question.

In the example given above, the trigram is 211, an even yin line above two odd yang lines. It occurs to me at this point that someone who knows the *Yijing* (in English translation, anyway) would be alarmed at this result. Yin lines predominate! Something evil is going to happen! In fact, the *Yijing* takes this trigram to be weak, but the *Ling Qi Jing* is more subtle in its understandings of the concept. Yin and yang are neither good nor evil. Each has its appropriate season. Each can stand for positive or negative forces in different situations. Do not waste time at this point calculating the positions of yin and yang, but turn immediately to the poem you have cast.

INTERPRETING THE TEXT

The first thing you must understand, and respect, concerning the text you hold in your hands is that it is a living entity. The ancients understood—as we seem to have forgotten—that in entrusting words to ink or to stone, those words are not killed but given a life of their own. Like other living beings, the text is not changeless but evolving. Over the course of its life, the *Ling Qi Jing* has emerged to speak most clearly during times of dire crisis and tumultuous potential; first, when China was divided into competing satrapies in the third and fourth centuries A.D., and again in the twentieth century.

The re-emergence of the *Ling Qi Jing* in our own time can be traced to the discovery by Aurel Stein and Paul Pelliot early in this century of a cache of religious texts in the Buddhist grottoes of Dunhuang, a city on the ancient caravan routes in the desert regions of far northwestern China. Among the Buddhist scrolls were many of the Daoist religion, and, among these, four copies of the *Ling Qi Jing*. While the majority of Chinese scholars recognize that these unique manuscripts would otherwise have perished, some still call the removal of the texts an act of robbery. But one thing is certain, the preservation of Dunhuang manuscripts in the major libraries of Europe led eventually to worldwide interest in the Daoist religion and renewed study of the Daoist canon by both Asian and Western scholars. Manuscript copies of the *Ling Qi Jing* were taken by Stein to London, by Pelliot to Paris, and, somewhat later, the Daoist canon, with its own version of the *Ling Qi Jing*, was published in Shanghai. The book you hold in your hands traces its parentage to all of these texts. For how it came into my hands, see the section "About the Author" at the end of this book.

READING THE POEMS: This is the heart of the Spirit Tokens system of guidance. The book is in the form of a four-line verse for each "fortune" cast. The choice of poetry is a conscious one. Poetry is "crystallized language"—verbal communication in its purest, most simplified form. Nothing causes us to think so deeply as the task of analyzing a poem, particularly when we know that the poem is somehow about us. The commentators have aided us in this process of analysis with their own interpretations, but finally, it is only the person who asks the question who is able to properly apply the poem. Read the poem several times, pondering its possible relevance for the problem that brought you to cast the tokens before turning to the commentators for further guidance.

USING THE COMMENTARIES: There are three traditional commentaries upon which I have drawn to help you interpret the verse you have cast. These will be signalled in the text as follows:

HE: He Chengtian (370-447) was a well-known scholar, official, mathmetician, and practitioner of numerical divination. He was able to live to a venerable age in an era of turmoil and early death, a feat made all the more remarkable by his continuous official service under two dynasties. His biography celebrates his excellent advice in all sorts of situations and outlines the sad fate of those, including an emperor of the second dynasty he served, who did not listen to him. Despite his reputation, his comments seem to me rather cut and dried. I have included his advice only sparingly.

YAN: Yan Youming, reputed to be a scholar of the early fourth century, is unknown in other sources. Yan's commentary is very useful in determining the play of forces underlying the construction of each verse.

JIE: The *jie,* or explanation, is unsigned. It was certainly composed by the eleventh century at the latest, since it is already present in Dunhuang manuscripts of the *Ling Qi Jing.* This commentary seems

24

to draw together the insights of He and Yan in a way that I have found particularly useful for the modern reader. In addition, it often focuses on the forces of the trigram underlying the verse. I have included this information when it seemed useful.

KASHIWA: In a few cases where I thought I had something to add, based on my own experiences and my heavily annotated copy of the text, I have added my own commentary. Usually, though, I have confined my remarks to interpreting for the modern reader of English what the traditional commentators had to say. I intend my commentaries primarily to encourage you to add your own.

A NOTE ON THE TRANSLATION: This is not a scholarly translation. In fact, it is not a direct translation of the text at all, except in the case of the poems which I thought should be rendered as closely to the original as possible, so long as the result was immediately accessible to a modern reader of English. The poems and your interpretations of them are, finally, the only matter of importance to the Spirit Tokens method of divination. From the traditional commentaries to the text I have selected and interpreted freely. My defense of this procedure, if one is required, is simply this: The early commentators were interpreting the Spirit Tokens for their culture and time; I am doing so for mine.

I have thus "used" them, as they "used" the work of others, to help begin the process of interpretation of the poems and the trigrams for my intended readers. For their cultural biases, I have substituted my own—that of a late twentieth-century resident of the United States. Encountering my "reading" of the commentaries, you will at any rate substitute your own "reading" of mine. What is finally important is not that either of us fully understand what the text originally meant to those of medieval China, but that it come alive to work its special brand of magic again in our own day.

Those interested in a scholarly study on the Spirit Tokens might consult Carole Morgan, "An Introduction to the *Lingqijing*," *Journal of Chinese Religions*, 21 (1993), pp. 97-120.

Spirit Tokens
of the
Ling Qi Jing

Trigrams
000–044

FLOODING DARKNESS
The Imageless

Darkness spreads without signs;
Portents have not yet taken shape.
If you move now, there will be cause for regret.
Retreat and protect your purity.

YAN: The formless takes on form, and form returns to formlessness—this is the eternal pattern of heaven and earth, yin and yang. There is hidden potential here, capable of all things, but now is not the time to act; it is the time to withdraw, protecting and nurturing your vital energies.

JIE: Before the beginning, yin and yang were still completely mixed and there was no way to fathom the shapes that were to come. Preserve this original purity—it is the key to all attainment. You may hear of sorrows but not be sorrowful; perceive joy, but not be joyful.

KASHIWA: This is the sign of the Dao, the formlessness that precedes all existence. Non-intervention (*wu wei*) is appropriate now.

NURTURING
Protecting Existence

Brilliant and luminous is heaven above;
Shining down on earth below.
Transforming and nurturing all forms of life,
It opens wide the doors for you.
All affairs are now manifest.
Each looks to the other in anticipation.

YAN: Heaven working together with earth is a sign of birth, nurturance, and growth.

JIE: When the light of heaven shines on earth below, there is growth. When growth begins to flourish, all things look upon one another. Everything begun in a propitious season will not only start smoothly, but also grow to fullness.

KASHIWA: This is the second in a series of five trigrams (000–004) that deal with the evolution of things in the world from the formelss, shapeless Dao that underlies all. You can most influence the outcome at this stage in the development of events.

GOOD EARTH
Contentment with Riches

When the roots are set, the matter is already settled.
Thus people, too, reach their potential.
Drinking clear water, eating wholesome food;
They ensure long life and health.

HE: When you throw this trigram there will be some delay. Affairs have not yet reached fullness.

JIE: The basic groundwork has been laid. Everything is already decided. When you realize this, an auspicious response will result from your actions.

KASHIWA: You should read the entire series of trigrams from 000 to 004 to understand where you are now in the development of events. Contemplate the direction of change. At this stage, all you can properly do is nourish positive forces.

OO3

ESTABLISHING AN OUTLOOK
Forming the Feminine

Affairs flourish when ability comes into full play.
The heroine takes her stand.
The sage and wise will save the world,
The patterns they establish accord with the
  principles of Nature.

YAN: This is a sign of hidden abilities coming into full play. Creativity rises from a firm foundation in the basics. This is the work of the heroine in each of us.

JIE: The fullness of yang energies in the earth, or feminine, position forms a firm basis for accomplishing affairs. Above there is no obstruction.

KASHIWA: This is a time for action and positive intervention (*you wei*).

APPROACHING DEATH
The Fullness of Yin

Nurturing life encompasses the approach to death—
A ritual cycle pure and full.
Filial descendants with decorated staffs,
Their clothing simple and reverential.

YAN: Every being receives the energy of heaven and thereby takes form. In so doing, every being enters the natural cycle that ends with death and the return to earth. The rituals of death clarify for each filial descendent this covenant with the natural cycle. Thus the text says "Nurturing life encompasses the approach to death."

JIE: This trigram reminds you of the natural cycle of life and death. With regard to what you have asked, struggle against such eternal verities is not warranted.

KASHIWA: Once again, non-intervention (*wu wei*) is called for. Read trigram 000. The death of a tree in the forest makes way for the growth of new shoots.

EMERGING YANG
The Light of Heaven

The light of heaven spreads over all below;
Sun and moon issue their luminescence.
This is a source of nourishment for all life;
All beings find sufficiency therein.

HE: All matters, even the most insignificant, are worthy of careful consideration—even the nurturing light of the sun and the moon, which we experience all the time without thinking.

JIE: The single yang in the center of this trigram is the symbol of sun, moon, and brilliance. There are prospects with regard to what you seek, but you must be patient and thoughtful.

OII

REVERENCE AND CAUTION
Brilliant Virtue

Brilliant virtue blocks perversity;
Affairs move in response to hidden triggers.
The wise one will cautiously begin;
The sage defends against the smallest sign.

YAN: Although the top position is blank, the yang energies are sufficient to make manifest their power. In all things follow the seasons in your actions and be aware of the smallest sign that things might be amiss.

HE: In all things you should seek for the hidden trigger that sets events in motion; then you will achieve your will.

JIE: As you begin, carefully consider all possible consequences of your actions. You must now be alert to even the slightest of signs, and be fully cognizant of the times in order for what you ask to turn out the way you wish.

OI2

GOD'S WAY
The Results of Virtue

Heaven and earth have the same motive force,
Which moves through yin and yang phases.
Its affairs are vast,
From the west down to the east;
Going, coming, moving, resting,
It is difficult to follow along.

YAN: When heaven and earth first opened to one another, vegetation began to grow. Such powerful forces do not lightly reveal their traces. What you seek will be difficult to bring into being.

HE: Your will is great but your goal is difficult to achieve. Don't count on it.

JIE: Still, this is a good sign for beginning new enterprises.

LACK OF RESOLUTION
Demon Doubt

Fox-cautious, hesitating,
No resolve in mind.
Advancing, you have no hope;
Retreating, you should remain true.

YAN: This is a sign of movement, conflict, and irresolution. There is no response within or without. With the patterns hidden, it is best not to move, but to withdraw and maintain your integrity.

HE: It is not clear to me whether you should advance or retreat. All that is clear is that it will be difficult to get what you seek.

JIE: There seems to be nothing for you to do, so your fear rises. There is no defense now against evil forces. There is only pure yang here, no yin. With regard to what you have asked, maintain a prudent stillness now.

PERVERSE FLATTERY
Hidden Doubts

Going against heaven,
Rebelling against the Lord,
He doesn't follow ordained patterns
But unrestrainedly flatters those above.
All about gnash their teeth.

YAN: There is no heaven position above and only a weak yang line below, so that the massed yin obscures and hides. Evil people avoid straight speech. There is flattery, cursing, and illogicality.

HE: Although they may offer flattery, everyone secretly despises those who are self-indulgent.

JIE: Avoid selfishness. There is willful perversity here. All is unpropitious.

KASHIWA: At this time, you should take stock of your own motives.

HARVEST
Paired Yang

Heaven and earth open fully to one another;
All existence flourishes in between.
The matter has just been decided:
It is the fullness of harvest-time.

YAN: This trigram is like Emerging Yang (010), which you should also consult, though the process is just a bit more advanced.

HE: You should not be willful or in a hurry.

JIE: Here human endeavour is about to receive its ultimate reward. Go slowly.

021

REMORSE
Admitting Transgressions

Above and below reversed;
Nothing you do seems fitting.
To the west you turn, then to the east;
There is nothing to pursue.

YAN: Something you have long desired will not go as you planned, since yin and yang forces are mixed and confounded. What you do will not benefit you, what you seek is not harmonious.

JIE: The first line of the poem means that the weak overcomes the strong in you, and the last that you have lost sight of your desires. Everything then turns against you. You should be cautious. Meditate on that which you asked, and strengthen your own resolve.

THE BEGINNINGS OF VIRTUE
Gazing into the Pit

Contemplating deeply, your thoughts fly off;
Sitting in safety, you worry about dangers.
You think: "Though there are no troubles today,
Everything will fall apart eventually."
Hey! Just keep to the path.
Don't deceive yourself!

YAN: Sometimes when you focus too deeply on your own safety and peace of mind, you undermine your efforts.

HE: You need to deeply contemplate this matter. What seems positive may not be so in the end.

JIE: Always weak and worried about your safety, you will certainly fall into debilitating misfortune. Walking the right path is finally the only way to maintain your good position. If a baby were content with what it had, how could it ever learn to walk? On the other hand, blind activity will only lead to defeat.

023

MEETING WITH LUCK
Fearful and Respectful

Virtue erases the unpropitious;
With fear and trembling, revere it!
Though now hidden and contingent,
Luck and position will come.

YAN: Your virtue is sufficient to drive off the unpropitious and eventually bring luck into your life. There will be small irritations in everything, but a large reward is at stake.

JIE: Your inner force is naturally such that you shouldn't even have asked.

KASHIWA: We are often most worried about outcomes once we have done everything we can humanly do. This is a time to trust in the rewards you will certainly receive for your efforts.

SNEAK THIEF
The Apex of Yin

Sneak thieves are plotting,
It's no good to wait until later.
Even if you temporarily defer your goals,
The results will be less than grand.

YAN: Drawing this trigram, you will find dark forces at work. Put your plan into action now or it will be too late.

HE: Get it done now and it will go as you wish.

JIE: Things you begin to plan now will go well at first, but later may meet with catastrophe.

KASHIWA: The course of action you contemplate will be beset with hidden difficulties. Be aware of them before you proceed.

HUMAN AFFAIRS
The Three Yang

Human endeavour has barely begun;
Future prospects are bright.
The one who stays will be enriched;
The one who goes will reach the goal.

YAN: Although there seems to be no outside aid, the matter can still be accomplished.

JIE: A fullness of yang energies occupies the central position. This calls for human strength applied in all directions. The heaven and earth lines are thereby brought into balance. Such careful applications of your energies will always bring propitious results.

A FORTUNATE POSITION
Primal Blessings

Going out the door, you meet with fortune—
A suitable companion for Goodness.
The bright pearl shines at night,
So you never get lost.

YAN: This is a fortunate sign—especially for business ventures.

JIE: Line one means that you will meet with a companion. Line three means that though it is dark, you will not be blind.

032

PROPITIOUS
Peace

When Heaven dissolves and the earth ceases,
The wise one still holds her place.
Travellers return, the ill are cured;
How infinitely easy it all is.

YAN: The good person is still and maintains her own, so all things return to her as to their source.

JIE: For those drawing this trigram, remember not to rush things. All will come in its time.

KASHIWA: Because the Ling Qi Jing is concerned with helping us see the progress of events from their very beginnings to fullness, it often warns of the dangers of complacency when all seems to be going as we wish. Here, however, it reminds us to recognize blessings and to rejoice when our efforts bring good results.

GATHERED FROM AFAR
Protecting Your Life

The phoenix holding a jewel in its beak
Alights in the corner of my yard,
Bringing fortune to me;
Dispelling disharmony for me.

YAN: When the heaven position is empty, only the strongest yang can fill the breach. This is a very auspicious sign. The phoenix is a blessed sign. The jewel it carries is a divine treasure, signifying your will to achieve what you seek.

JIE: The way is made smooth for you now. Only if you are seeking rain is this a bad sign.

034

NEGATIVE TENDENCIES
Using Wisdom

When rulers are contentious,
The subjects are bent and bowed.
When an enlightened one rules,
She distinguishes purple from red.

YAN: If you have no position, now is the time to seek one. Everything else also falls into its logical pattern.

HE: If what you seek comes from a right heart, it is inevitable that those who oppose you will submit to the correctness of your course.

JIE: This is a good sign for those in all walks of life. The eternal patterns are restored.

PROTECTING YOURSELF
A Fullness of Yin

Spectral vapors have not yet formed;
The miasmal forces have not yet taken shape.
Now is the time to protect yourself—
Remain secure within your gates.

YAN: Yin forces are full in the central position, but there is nothing on either side to respond to them yet. It is best for you to make preparations now, before inimical forces have had the time to join ranks.

JIE: You should retreat, maintain secrecy, and protect your vital forces. Stillness is often the most appropriate action.

041

REPRIEVED
The Dragon Rises

The hidden dragon is soon to ascend;
Mysterious clouds already rise.
All under the sky is covered with grace.
First it looks bad, but joy is coming.

YAN: At first things are not so good, but then all responds to the wondrous blessings swelling from the earth into the heavens. When the dragon is about to rise and fly across the heavens, mists rise to meet it. Watch for them.

JIE: It will be joyous, as if those initial setbacks had never occurred. This is a highly auspicious sign.

042

BREAKING COVER
Decline

Heaven's dragon roars in rage;
The thunder god beats his drum.
Rising clouds bring rain,
Which freely flows to the earth below.

YAN: Since this trigram is purely yin, you have reached a time when there is no response from without and you are unable to dispel misfortune. There is envy and stinginess.

HE: In the face of over powering natural forces, affairs cannot be settled with certainty.

JIE: Line four indicates that it is now hard to rise up. This trigram is only good if you have asked for rain.

043

FLEEING THE WORLD
Unpropitious

Knaves get their way,
Sages lose theirs.
Abandoning my house,
I enter the deep grass.

YAN: Maintain your virtues but withdraw. This is a time when goodness is obstructed. In such situations, the sages of old would leave their homes to dwell in the wilderness, strengthening their resolve and awaiting the proper time.

KASHIWA: There are times when all of your best efforts are of no avail. Even so, there is work for you to do. Despair is never a positive strategy.

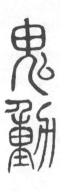

GHOSTLY MOVEMENT
Applying Magic

Even when two ghosts live together,
There is still only hunger and emptiness.
They might wish to enter the door of the living,
But fear the holy talismans.

YAN: This is a sign that you are troubled by the influences of the dead. You have no spiritual center. Only by studying religious books—the records of humanity's attempts to deal with the departed—will you be able to eradicate these influences.

HE: You should carry out meritorious actions. Do good deeds to remove inharmonious influences.

JIE: While it seems there is nothing to rely on, there are higher powers. You ask about a troubling matter. Find some spiritual support.

Spirit Tokens
of the
Ling Qi Jing

Trigrams
100–144

LACK OF CLARITY
Heaven's Origin

With the initial stirrings,
Before anything was formed,
Light had not yet formed to show
Movement in the primal murk—
This is when the revolutions of fortune began,
Before there were even events to move.

YAN: One represents the origins of the cosmos. All things began in primordial unity. There is a period of gradual development ahead. Contemplate trigrams 100, 200, 300, and 400 in sequence.

JIE: Before anything had begun to move, there was no way to fathom which direction would be taken. What you ask will not now be achieved. It is too early. Everything is calm and expectant.

101

SLIGHT LOSSES
Seeking Stability

When climbing a tree to gather mulberry leaves,
He fell to the ground, his body stiffened.
The eastern neighbor has a drug,
Someone run to get it!
In this way a miraculous cure
Removes all injury and harm.

YAN: Your grasping for things is making you ill. Good fortune lies in letting go. Though letting go is terrifying, in this way you will make progress and find help.

JIE: It is dangerous to ascend to the heights. There is danger and harm in all forms of acquisitiveness. It is good to make recompense, but better to make full payment beforehand.

INITIAL HARMONY
The Beginnings of Peace

Like a newlywed bride,
You are not yet accustomed to your home.
Only through your own efforts
Will there be a family.

YAN: The yin and yang are harmonious here, though there is as yet no center. Things will respond in time. Much depends on your effort now.

JIE: Love is not mature just because the sentiment is mutual. There is no obstruction, however, and what is far will be brought near.

KASHIWA: What looks like a harmonious outcome still requires effort. Continue to work in the direction you have chosen.

103

WITHOUT TILLING
Wasteland

The land is elevated, the stones hard;
You raise your head to blame heaven,
Yet you haven't brought a plow.
No wonder the earth is barren.

YAN: Fertile ground signifies nothing. You must plow and sow.

HE: You must seek properly for what you wish. Actually this is no more than an ordinary state of affairs—luck plays no part here.

JIE: Things are rough and you do not know what to do. There is division and no growth. It seems as if you labor in vain, but don't blame heaven.

104

A HAUNTING
Wasting Away

There are demons in the house,
Sitting side by side.
You seek for things you have lost.
There is no water, no heat.
Heavenly spirits, earthly powers,
All watch for human transgressions.

YAN: With nothing to mediate the yin and yang powers there is contention and aimless striving. Worries fill the gap.

HE: Be careful that you are not trying to mix fire and water. You should examine yourself for fault within.

JIE: It is already over. Why do you ask?

110

THE BITTER SEASON
Dessication

Toiling along in poverty,
No gate to call your own.
Hobbled in both coming and going,
You own not enough earth to stick a nail in.

YAN: There is no harmony here. Strength remains outside and has no support from within. Thus there is no stability and you hobble, struggling in spiritual poverty.

HE: There is no help for you at home, thus "you own not enough earth to stick a nail in."

JIE: The two upper lines of the trigram have no foundation below. This is a sign of loneliness, cold, poverty, and lack of foundation. Seek a basis for your actions.

III

ASCENDING
The Grand Concourse

Moving from small to large,
There is no disturbance of order.
From below, ascending to the heights,
One arrives at wealth and influence.
Appropriate to venture forth;
Inappropriate to withdraw.

YAN: For those in a lesser position desiring greater, this is highly auspicious; for those in a greater position envious of the lesser, this could lead to danger. All sorts of overt action on your part will be rewarded, but you should not be secretive or engage in plots.

HE: It is a time to be open, not hidden.

JIE: Line one reflects the fact that this is a sign of nascent yang energies. Do not hide your abilities. When three people are of the same mind, travelling together is appropriate.

112

GRADUAL HARMONY
Receiving Blessings

With self-satisfaction, the enterprise spreads;
What you produce now brings returns.
Both wealth and honor are yours,
Yet you fall short of that desired outcome.

YAN: Still your passions and settle your will; all things come when it is time. If you wish for a speedy outcome, you will be disappointed.

JIE: If you do not expect too much from others, you will be gratified. Remember that unbridled ambition is repugnant. You should be content with your allotted portion and refrain from grasping. If you hear of sorrow do not be sorrowful.

KASHIWA: It seems like we always want more, doesn't it?

PROSPERITY
Auspicious Events

Lofty, towering, bright and shining—
Your home is filled with gold and silks.
When one is materially endowed, all things may
* be achieved;*
You reap even where you have not sown.

YAN: When one is blessed with material prosperity, desire is unseemly…and unnecessary. Why are you asking this?

JIE: The bounties of the material world are great. What you ask for will come to you naturally; make sure that you need it.

KASHIWA: "Behold the fowls of the air: for they sow not, neither do they reap, nor gather into barns; yet your heavenly Father feedeth them." (Matthew 6:26)

114

PROFUSION
The Passage to Harmony

Having bestowed wealth and honor,
The Way of Heaven tends to reverse course.
Follow the ups and downs of fated cycles;
Shrink and expand with the times,
Then your rewards will exceed all count.

YAN: The rich and famous should remember the poor and lowly. If one reaching the heights cannot learn to be humble and unassuming, a reverse is imminent. If you do not move contrary to the trends of the time, you will be successful.

JIE: When anything reaches fullness, decline inevitably follows. The time of greatest achievement is the time of utmost danger. Learn to follow the twists and turns of fate with grace. If you do not go against the natural seasons of things and are content with your portion, you will prosper and achieve your desires.

JOY
The Partner

Husband and wife are close,
There is no "other" for them.
Sitting together, knee to knee,
They experience only deep contentment.

YAN: The brittle and the pliant respond to one another. This is a sign of joy. Everything is now in harmony.

JIE: Even though this trigram has no bottom line, the yang and yin complement one another. Everything is harmonious in small matters, but be cautious in large matters.

KASHIWA: Notice that the poem says "knee to knee" rather than "side by side." Harmonious relationships require negotiation, mutual understanding, and equality.

DELIGHTING IN THE WAY
Startled by Joy

Hard without, pliant within;
Through merging these two, one is complete.
Nurture your nature, protect your life,
And carefree you will roam with the spirits.

YAN: That which you seek is unreasonable and excessive. You should strive for balance, since it is only through a balanced approach to life that you may protect yourself.

HE: Don't force yourself forward. Now is the time to work on your own strengths and weaknesses.

JIE: "Hard without, pliant within" means that you find it too easy to agree with others. You should plan carefully and be cautious in action now. Consolidate your personal and spiritual powers before moving ahead. Difficulties caused by things you hear are the result of people spreading falsehoods. Find your own truth within. In this way you will find greater fulfillment than you thought possible.

122

TERRIFIED
A Minor Risk

To crow at dawn, the cock
Ascends to the roof and stretches its neck.
The hen below the wall
Is startled by a fox.
If the cock stops crowing and leaps down,
Loss of life may be averted.

YAN: In whatever you undertake now there will at first be difficulty and confusion. It may look as if there is no help for your situation, but in the end there will be no further cause for worry. Don't panic!

JIE: The cock and the hen here refer to the fact that the pliant and flexible cannot triumph when the hard and unyielding is placed above. There is a tendency here to push your abilities too far, to the detriment of your weaker attributes. Recognize the danger signs that arise when you overextend yourself. Use your strengths to shore up your weaknesses and you will find in your current weakness, paradoxically, a source of strength.

123

ABUNDANT HARVESTS
Well-Chosen Fields

In the first quarter of the first month,
The Year Star is at the Great Bridge.
The east wind breaks up the ice—
Now is the time to choose your fields.
At the end of the year the harvest is full—
This joy is hard to match.

YAN: You choose appropriate actions at the appropriate times—this can lead to nothing but success.

JIE: Human actions need to accord with the greater movements of the natural world. If there is harmony above, there will be abundance and blessings below. Still, you must not expect an immediate response. In fact, it will seem that rewards are slow in coming. Wait for the natural outcome.

KASHIWA: The "year star" is Jupiter. Its crossing of the Milky Way comes at the Chinese constellation "Great Bridge."

A MINOR TRANSGRESSION
Limited Achievements

Disaster arises from below:
Be prudent and proper toward those under you.
When hidden plotters band together,
You may finally want to swing into action.

YAN: You need to be cautious in all of your actions, so as not to call down on yourself great misfortune. There are those who seek to upset your plans. Exclusive absorption in your own goals and desires make you especially vulnerable. You put yourself in a weak position through self-aggrandizement.

JIE: Your strength is isolated and vulnerable. Forces that have labored on your behalf may no longer do so. If you do not learn to work with and for others, you will learn to your detriment the efficacy of concerted action. Act to restore harmony now before it is too late.

130

FOLLOWING IN ORDER
Accomplishment

Having achieved my station,
Things follow according to my will.
With fixed mind and untroubled heart
Wealth and rank follow in order.
Felicitations and blessings
Benefit me for a long time.

YAN: Three yang occupy the center line and everything follows in order.

JIE: Yang forces are perfectly propitious here. Everything sits in its proper position. There is no conflict above or below, guaranteeing luck and advantage. Further striving may be counterproductive.

FULFILLED ASPIRATIONS
Satisfaction

When you have clearly achieved your desires
And have acted at the right times,
Your material wants are fulfilled
And you lack not the means to push ahead.

YAN: Now that you have all you set out to achieve, why do you further burden yourself with the delusion that your material needs are not met? When the great king of antiquity, King Wen, was about to go into battle, he suddenly discovered that his shoelaces were untied. Looking to his attendants, he saw only righteous warriors, so he tied them himself. This is the attitude you should foster!

JIE: Everything is going in your favour. It is a time for great accomplishment. Why are you even asking about this now?

132

IN DUE COURSE
Incipient Greatness

Earlier, things did not go as you wished.
Now you learn to follow your will.
Everything follows a pattern;
You know what you must do.

YAN: Begin by determining what it is that you really want. Your desires must be based on a strong sense of morality and uprightness. Then, when you have brought everything into harmony, all will be well.

JIE: In your earlier thinking about this problem, you betrayed an inner weakness. You were hobbled by selfishness and the mistaken belief that everything centered on you. You now have the strength to act in an appropriately unselfish fashion. Do not serve the self. Know your place in the greater scheme of things and act in the full light of this understanding. If you are able to do this, the consequences will be magnificent.

133

ACHIEVEMENT THROUGH SKILL
A Good Augury

Numerous and bustling, the talented ones—
The bright light of their many virtues shines.
Seeing one another, they rejoice together.
There will be joy everlasting.

YAN: If you reveal your true abilities, someone in a position of authority is sure to help you. You will come into full strength at the end of the year—and in more than one area.

JIE: The phrase "Numerous and bustling, the talented ones" means that there is someone (or something) in a higher position that they follow. "Seeing one another, they rejoice together" means that through unified action they will be ennobled. If someone in a lower station draws this trigram, it means that he will be honored for his talents and that a good friend will aid him. If it is someone in a higher position, it means that she should be aware of the benefits of joint action.

134

ROAMING FREELY
The Joy of Travel

Mounting a dragon, spurring a charger,
One travels to the four corners of the world.
Happily giving rein to one's thoughts,
One finds boundless joy in travel.

YAN: If you follow your heart's desires, there will be nothing, in any direction, that you do not achieve. The *Yijing* states "When it is time, mount the six dragons to ride to heaven," and "The mare is categorized with the things of the earth; it travels the earth without bound."

JIE: "Mounting a dragon, spurring a charger" means that those things under one's control function as they should. "One travels to the four quarters of the world" means that there is nothing to block you. Now is the time for action.

DEMON MINIONS
The Ranks of the Outcast

Food does not enter his mouth;
Breath does not issue from his nose.
Breast knotted in anguish,
No sleep he knows.

YAN: The assembled yin powers lodge within, contravening the nascent yang. This brings stress and injury.

HE: You should blame yourself. Why do you rush to blame fate?

JIE: One yang and four yin indicate that your desires may not proceed. "Breast knotted in anguish" indicates that the source of trouble is inside. You are divided on this question. This is a sign of worry and illness. Guard against whatever it is that wastes your powers. Be particularly watchful lest despair defeat you.

141

VEXATIONS
Standing Alone

Alone above, orphaned below—
Evil has designs on you.
The illness of the heart and stomach
Cannot be fully eradicated.
Wait until the height of spring,
Then things will begin to go your way.

YAN: Your constant worry and fear has been harmful. It would be beneficial to consult someone in a position of authority. Then you may proceed with caution.

JIE: "Alone above, orphaned below" refers to the fact that full-blown yin occupies the central position, blocking the two yang forces. There is something, perhaps something within you, that is keeping you from fulfilling your desires. You need to maintain your own rectitude, prepare appropriately, and bide your time. This is like trigram 121, which you also should consult, but the situation now is somewhat worse. If you act appropriately, all will eventually go your way.

THE POWER OF CAUTION
The Bandit

As heaven and earth unfold,
The petty man sometimes has his way.
The prohibitions are not enforced;
A robber spies on my dwelling.

YAN: With this trigram it is very important that you uphold rectitude and not engage exclusively in your own affairs. You may lose something, but ultimately you will regain it and more.

JIE: "Heaven and earth unfold" refers to the fact that the rules by which we may live rightly have already been made manifest. "A robber spies on my dwelling" means that the house is closed up. Just as robbers cannot see in, so we have failed to look out to observe the laws inherent in nature. The wise person's failings are the villain's joy. You should begin to act with rectitude. Stop plundering both yourself and others. Maintain your home and the earth's produce.

143

DESTROYING THE ENEMY
Giving Orders

The sovereign's commands govern affairs,
Eradicating the evil and violent.
Search out spears, array your lances,
Great is the result to be achieved.

YAN: It is a time for driving out evil. Those who have been dominant will now be defeated. The lesser will overcome the greater. Those who strive only to hold on to their own will defeat themselves.

JIE: Yin is here encompassed within, which means that your desires should be righteous. "Search out spears, array your lances" means to attack illness and wrong. Though your desires have been blocked, through concerted action the blockage may be cleared away, as long as your desires are appropriate.

144

DEFEAT
The General is Lost

Wolves and tigers howl
In a steady, drizzling rain.
Now that the battle is lost,
Both weak soldiers and brave
Are set on by bandits—
Many are those who perish.

YAN: Destroying "this" to benefit "that" is not logical. Everything now is difficult. Your course becomes weaker day by day and enemies are now everywhere. These obstacles are difficult to overcome.

JIE: "Wolves and tigers" and "drizzling rain" all refer to the fact that important details have long been ignored and now emerge all at once to threaten from every side. Force will do you no good. Try withdrawing. Bathe yourself in the rain.

Spirit Tokens
of the
Ling Qi Jing

———————

Trigrams
200–244

SHIFTING STREAMS
Extreme Subtlety

Images were first established in the heavens.
Primordial energies floated and drifte.d.
Not yet enough to be called something,
They flowed freely to the east and west.

YAN: This is the stage of creation following that described in trigram 100. Newly arising forces drift with seeming aimlessness. There is no stability. In such a situation, you may not be able to move according to your own will, but possibilities will form.

JIE: This is the most subtle moment of an evolving process. There seems nothing on which to base yourself, since everything shifts and flows. Study this moment of creativity.

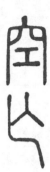

EMPTINESS AND LOSS
Disappointments

Jumping into a lake to chop trees,
Or climbing a mountain to catch fish—
Just a waste of time and energy;
Your hands and mouth are still empty.

YAN: Everything is upside down. Nothing you attempt in this uncertain situation pays off.

JIE: Lines one and two mean you are moving in the wrong direction. You certainly will not achieve what you are after in this way. Rethink your goals. Try another direction.

KASHIWA: All your efforts seem to have achieved are results precisely contrary to those you intended. It is extremely important to act thoughtfully at this juncture.

202

INHARMONIOUS
Two Halves

Two spouses without mate;
They have fought with their mates and live apart.
Now they stay away even from each other.
Now they divide their lodgings in half.

YAN: Your will is divided on this question. This is an exceedingly bad sign.

HE: If you have two conflicting ideas on this, it is because you have pretended to shift ground, but have not fully done so. Examine your motives.

KASHIWA: That old enemy indecision often appears when we have not examined the situation carefully enough. Indecision will also lead to conflict with others. If you wish to be alone, do so.

203

OUT OF PRACTICE
Wasted Labor

One person follows another,
Wanting to avoid some danger;
One after another they fall into a well—
Now who's to pull them out?

YAN: In trying to avoid hidden danger you have lost your way. Your energies and intelligence are wasted if you do not use them at the proper time. You brought this on yourself.

HE: There seems no way you can actively work to achieve what you want right now.

JIE: You lack self-confidence. Your abilities are sufficient. Why do you delay?

204

RADICAL CHANGE
Debilitating Darkness

Snow flurries swirl,
Soaking my garments.
The north wind blows me on,
I cannot return home.

YAN: Snow covers the return road. There is trouble now.

HE: Nothing proceeds smoothly now. You should be especially cautious of deceit and flattery.

JIE: It is always wise to shun activities that will harm you.

KASHIWA: This event is too fully formed. All you can do now is wait out the storm, watching for the incipient signs of change as they unfold.

DELAYED GRATIFICATION
Smooth at Last

You entrusted someone with a matter—
Each day you wait for word.
Only today have you heard
That the news is good.
Although the matter has been delayed
Finally you get your wish.

YAN: The matter you ask about will become further complicated before you receive help. If you share the problem with someone, it will be resolved satisfactorily. But if you isolate yourself, you will find you cannot do it alone. While you find yourself without help, you should delay things for a while.

HE: If you confide in someone the question that occupies your mind, things will work out as you wish.

JIE: Everything seems difficult at first. Don't rush.

SHAMANS
The Divine Protectors

When Grand Unity marshals his troops,
The Jade Woman stands by his side.
Here is Wu Xian, Master of Transcendence,
To drive away misfortune.

YAN: There are hidden forces at work here. "Grand Unity" is the Lord of Heaven, and the "Jade Woman" his primary assistant. Wu Xian was a renowned shaman of the Shang Dynasty [1520 to 1030 B.C.]. This trigram betokens the uprooting of evil and the arrival of good fortune.

JIE: Though the yin force in this trigram occupies the superior position, the two yang forces unite to drive out perversity, so that the lone yin is converted and no longer stands in opposition. Though the situation now seems doubtful, your right actions will transform those who might have stood in the way. Some will now aid you. This is the glorious force of the intermediary Wu Xian, who was able to balance and control both yin and yang.

THE CURSE
Destruction Threatens

One husband, two wives:
Above and below, they urge one another along.
Yin forces control the yang;
The center gradually wastes away.

YAN: Hemmed in by two Jade Women, the Grand Unity of the preceding trigram is perverted and begins to waste away. This is a sign of sexual or sensual excess.

JIE: A person's vital forces are dissipated through immoderation and debauchery. Your power declines. When a single yang sinks between two yin, all are naturally weakened thereby. In your search for harmony in all things, you have perhaps forgotten that vitality is essential and have fallen into practices that, though seemingly productive, waste you. To avoid disaster, you need to renounce pleasure and harden your resolve.

AGAINST LICENTIOUSNESS
Adjusting Your Nature

The heavens blacken as clouds ascend;
Vital forces must arise from below.
The sage controls disorder;
Small people fear chastisement.

YAN: Your vitality, recently at low ebb, will begin to rise. Avoid violent action and all unpropitious elements will dissolve of themselves. This trigram calls for strict control of the self. If you can achieve such self-control, there will be difficulties at first, but great felicity is in store for you.

JIE: "The heavens blacken as clouds ascend" is the sign of the dragon rising from the abyss. Rectitude breaks through perversity and disorder like water bursting a dike. The sagely one controls disorder both within herself and without, while petty people loathe self-control and only act out of fear of punishment. This trigram is a bad sign only if you are planning some deceit or selfishness.

214

FLEEING TROUBLE
No Return

Fields laid waste, the earth barren;
The people have become refugees.
They await the fullness of harvest time
To return to their hearths and homes.

YAN: This is a fullness of yin that can no longer be blocked by yang.

HE: Although this trigram is inauspicious, there will be no harm. You must learn to be happy in your poverty and preserve stillness of spirit.

JIE: When the fields are laid waste and the earth is barren, there is nothing on which to depend. The perverse desires of the small man are finally unproductive. If you maintain the right way and persevere, you will certainly achieve your place in the scheme of things.

VEXATIONS AND PARTINGS
Caution

Although things are peaceful,
Still there is danger;
Although things are joyous,
Still there are vexations.
If you always worry about partings,
How do you expect to gain friends?

YAN: Two yin lines are paired, and there is no yang to contend with them or pair with them. Having upright desires, one often finds oneself seemingly without friends.

HE: There is a contradiction. If you have not been careful about the morality of the thing you ask, it will be difficult to achieve your desires.

JIE: "Although things are peaceful" means that your house is empty. "You always worry about partings" indicates that you find no one to join you in your pursuit. You have the will, but no one to be your partner or to depend on. If you achieve what you seek now, you may find yourself losing in the end.

HOARDING
Guard Against Greed

Burying gold, hoarding jade,
You announce your own worth.
But if your spiritual debts are not paid,
The gods will not grant you wealth.

HE: Those who rest secure in high positions and content themselves in their material wealth will undoubtedly bring down disaster upon themselves.

JIE: Burying gold is the same as hiding your talents or refusing to use your energies where they are needed. You are bound to be hurt by your greed if you do not reconsider.

REPOSE
The Ornamental Garden

The year is a good one, the season is right.
Cultivated fields stretch into the distance.
Peace reigns over all like majestic Mount Tai.
There will be no unseen reverses.

YAN: When the fields are cultivated to await the full-ness of harvest, there can finally be no ill fate for you. Your inner peace is immoveable, like the mighty Mount Tai, and you calmly survey your good work.

JIE: All are in accord, and as a result there are no contrary indications.

KASHIWA: If you have worked diligently and paid due attention to the unfolding of the seasons so that all your actions have been timely, there is noth-ing more to worry about.

223

HEAVEN-GRANTED POSITION
The Fullness of Fate

You receive your position under heaven,
As surely as the sun rises.
For those in lesser positions,
There is no way but up.

YAN: The double yin elements here indicate movement like the rising of the sun. You are very near to the fulfillment of your desires. It is not appropriate for you to remain in seclusion or to hide your talents. Now is the time to act!

HE: If that which you seek is of high moral purpose, you will reach your goal. This is not a time for selfish plotting.

RICHES
Smooth Sailing

As beneficial as a bubbling spring—
Though you draw water, it is not depleted.
That which you desire will come,
To be a never-ending source of happiness.

YAN: Wealth, both spiritual and material, is like a bubbling spring; when you draw from it, it is never depleted.

JIE: The line "as beneficial as a bubbling spring" points particularly to riches drawn from the earth. It is a sign that the fields you have chosen to cultivate are fertile indeed. If you do not act rashly, everything you seek will be granted. You will enjoy greatly the benefits of your long labours.

CONTENT WITH SUFFICIENCY
Great Achievements

Crossing into my fields
Rumbles a line of carts.
What treasures do they carry?
Gold and silver.
They bring me riches;
I will never fear poverty.

YAN: Yin occupies the top position and yang the center. Your wishes receive response from outside. This trigram is greatly propitious. What you ask for is easily achieved.

HE: Perhaps someone will bring you something or you will achieve riches through a request.

JIE: There is no question of poverty or worry concerning that which you have asked. There is great felicity, but if you have asked concerning your position, your possessions, or a job, you will find no benefit at home, only abroad.

231

FUTURE BENEFITS
Joy and Worry

There is sorrow in your heart;
You toss and turn sleeplessly.
You fear there is some calamity in store,
And the good times only make it worse.
Rejoice in your happinesses—
You will benefit greatly thereby.

JIE: In any undertaking hardship precedes accomplishment. But your worries are empty while your accomplishments are full.

KASHIWA: That you consult the *Ling Qi Jing* concerning this matter indicates that you are worrting needlessly over circumstances beyond your control. Take time to rejoice in what you have, then assess the situation again. Is the question you have asked really what is bothering you?

232

PEACE
Secret Concord

Above and below, all is at rest—
Do not let guile arise in your heart.
There is nothing at all to worry about.
Do not believe rumors.

YAN: Sometimes there is benefit even in those things that worry you the most.

JIE: Above and below are pliant and the center rules. If you remain firm in your convictions, all will join with you. The only danger you face now is from within. There will be forms and images to deceive you, but there is no harm in them. Maintain your good resolve.

233

AVOIDING EVIL
The Fullness of Virtue

Everyone loves me;
I drive off sorrows and calamities.
The rabid dog will not bite me;
The million negativities will not reach fruition!

YAN: For those with a positive attitude, everything is propitious—you will surely find others willing to help you. Even though yin clouds gather in the upper position, this will not endure against the strength of the yang forces below. Your strength will not flag—nurture it and worries will not assail you.

JIE: The yin in the upper position means that you should maintain a suitable modesty, but do not let that affect your confidence. You will thus be revered and those with talent will aid you, assuring that you do not come to harm. With the appropriate help, all will be achieved.

THE CATCH
Control Over Things

When Han Lu chased rabbits,
He never broke into a run.
With a snarling dog in front
And Han Lu behind,
The hare was hemmed in—
Not daring to flee.

YAN: This anecdote of the snarling dog and the rabbit which did not dare to run means that you need not exert so much effort to achieve your aspirations. Be steadfast but patient. There will be small gains at first and the goal will finally be won.

JIE: The greater yang in the middle indicates that this is a time for inner firmness. In this way, though petty people are often agile, they will be unable to contend with you. That which you asked for will be achieved, unless it is a matter of untying or dissolution.

AIDING THE ENDANGERED
Staying Within Bounds

The sage so exalted,
What is her shape?
Wise and good, responding to others—
First crying, then singing.

YAN: The sage differs from others in that, no matter what the situation, her refined nature shines forth so that she is honored by others. At first there are worries, but finally joy.

An alternate version of the poem reads:

Yesterday I went out on campaign
Bandits blocked my way.
A stray arrow struck me,
My eyes overflow with tears.

JIE: Going out on campaign and meeting disaster means that there are negative yin forces within. "Struck by a stray arrow" indicates that your vision is blocked. Whoever gets this trigram will be beset by trivial forces, perhaps lack of self-confidence. Be cautious that you do not injure yourself.

241

LOSS AND GAIN
The Second Chance

Sages and worthies succeed one another;
There is decline, but growth follows.
When melon vines twine thickly,
You must prune them for best growth.

YAN: Things seem to scatter in every direction, but the time of joining is at hand. Even though you are weak now, keep your will set on the right way and your strength will return; that which was disrupted will be continued.

JIE: The middle of this trigram reveals a fullness of yin. Reaching its apex, it must decline. "Melon vines twine thickly" means that your strength will begin to grow. The dangers are many, and petty people seem to prevail, but they will meet reversals. It is appropriate now to cut your losses, to reapportion your strengths, and to ready yourself for the season of growth.

AVOIDING DISASTER
Maintaining Stillness

When summer departs and autumn arrives,
Cold and frost begin to cause damage.
Beasts grow furry coats and hibernate;
Plants wither, drawing their life back into
* their roots.*

YAN: It is said "Summer is the time for production, autumn the time for storing away. When yang disperses, yin reaches its apogee." When it is time for the sage to rest in stillness, it is dangerous for her to labor to push matters forward.

JIE: "When summer departs and autumn arrives" is the season of yin growth. This is the time when even the wise find the way blocked. One who has drawn this trigram should now imitate the response of the natural world to the oncoming winter. You should withdraw, store away, and maintain stillness. It is not appropriate to advance. You are unlikely now to get what you seek.

243

ENLIGHTENMENT
Growth

When yin reaches its peak, it changes to yang,
Hibernating beasts begin to stretch.
A reprieve is granted to all under heaven;
Gongs and drums echo resoundingly.

YAN: Now is the season when the dark storehouses of nature release their bounty. All is propitious, except in matters pertaining to marriage, since yin and yang have not yet attained balance.

JIE: "When yin reaches its peak, it changes to yang" refers to inner changes. "Hibernating beasts begin to stretch" means that these changes have far-reaching consequence, like the thunder that arises from the earth in spring. "Gongs and drums echo resoundingly" alludes to the fact that the sound of your powerful virtues will spread abroad. For the sage, this is the time when the Way will flourish.

244

ILLNESS
Submerged Processes

A minor illness in the genitals;
You are rigid and full of fear.
Raise your head to survey the skies,
Lower your head in contrition.

YAN: There is trouble brought on by dark yin forces, perhaps by incontinence in sexual matters, but it will not worsen if dealt with properly. "Raise your head to survey the skies" means that you will not receive help from others. It seems that all you can do is worry, but it is not too late to correct and heal yourself.

JIE: When yin forces overcome you and you act lasciviously, you naturally worry about reversal, since you are only thinking of yourself. This is highly inauspicious.

Spirit Tokens
of the
Ling Qi Jing

Trigrams
300–344

300

UNSETTLED
The Shapes

Now heaven and earth have taken shape,
Humankind is formed.
Follow the energies above and below;
They still have not found their place.

YAN: This is the creative stage following on that described in trigrams 100 and 200, which you should also consult. This best describes the present developmental stage of human society: We have not yet found our place in the order of things, nor have we learned our places with regard to one another. While there is no ultimate catastrophe resulting from this, neither is there peace.

HE: There is a source for everything. If you think that you are doing as you please, you deceive yourself.

JIE: At first, all was tossed on chaotic waves of energy as tendencies established themselves. Choose your direction, but do not upset the creative flux.

301

WITHOUT MERIT
Fruitless Labor

Going east to pick medicinal herbs,
I ascend Mount Tai.
Failing to find those special plants,
I see only fragrant orchids.
Orchids have no special use,
So I return empty-handed.

YAN: Going to pick herbs and finding only orchids is a sign of empty beauty. Be cautious now of things that have beautiful names but no actual value; of things that seem joyful but bring no real joy; and of things that seem troublesome but are not really worth bothering about.

JIE: In the present mismatching of name and reality, it is difficult for you to take any positive action at all. Reconsider.

FLOODING
Difficulties

It has been drizzling, seemingly forever.
Floodwaters rise to the heavens.
People live in treetops;
No way to light a fire.

YAN: Yin and yang are in conflict. Your objective is endangered.

HE: This is a sign of impending chaos. It is not appropriate to do anything now.

JIE: If you get what you ask for now, it will spell disaster.

303

DROUGHT
Emptiness and Depletion

Blazing drought besets us,
Heaven and earth are scorched.
Ascend to heaven seeking a dragon;
Enter the earth looking for springs.
With fear and trembling,
All wait uneasily.

YAN: This is highly unpropitious. There is no response from above or below.

HE: During drought, it seems that heaven has turned against you. Add to this resentment among people, and it seems there is nowhere to turn.

JIE: Since the middle line of the trigram is empty and waiting to be filled, your energies now might best be directed toward other people. Proceed with extreme caution.

304

ASSAULTING THE DISTANT
Dispersal

They chase the fleeing bandits
All the way to the ocean.
It was my treasures the robbers took,
But the army leads off my oxen and sheep.

YAN: You are using strength and money to carry out a grand scheme that is not the least beneficial to you. Is it worth it?

HE: It is never a good idea to waste the resources of others in pursuit of your own goals. If you do take from others, be certain to thank and repay them.

JIE: This is a sign of loss. You may recover through much labor and expenditure.

310

FLOWING FORTUNE
Heaven Achieved

Having repeatedly met with disappointment,
Now you bump into greatness.
Not only this one time—
Fortune comes in a series.

YAN: The full yang line is on top. Nothing can assail you now. Good luck and blessings are on their way. This trigram means that at first things may move at cross-purposes—there may even be some cause for worry—but there will be no final hardship. You and your associates will benefit.

JIE: The two types of yang energy, above and below, do not contradict or block one another. Your will is in accord with natural principles, and this brings you felicity.

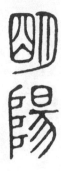

LUMINOUS YANG
Steady Progress

The employee, when the time comes,
Receives wages and then a pension.
Laboring diligently, sticking to the task,
Through her sincerity, she will not lose what is due.

YAN: A government functionary, one who takes care of the day-to-day matters of administration, receives a steady wage, no matter who is in office or what the season. This means that you should be assiduous in your work and not slacken in your endeavors. Avoiding both an excess of yin and a surplus of yang is the surest way to bring glory to yourself. Watch over those talents and material blessings that you are given and find your rightful place in society—this is the way to peace in all things.

JIE: There is glory in uprightness. In the service of natural processes there is great benefit. The sage's time is at hand; the time for service has arrived. There is appropriateness in what you seek. Real progress will result from your right action now.

312

HEAVEN'S AID
Finding the Road

Climbing high and gazing afar,
I see the crossroads of heaven.
The Jade Woman, a great sage,
Grants me a holy talisman;
Providing me with longevity
And protecting my health.

YAN: This is a sign of gain; something is to be expected from a woman. The spiritual and the mundane join—the feeling of power is like looking out over the world from atop a mountain. Meditate on this for a moment. There is a sign of supernatural response to your seeking. Your yin and yang components achieve harmony. Also, the lower part of the trigram responds to yin powers—you will find a soul-mate when necessary.

313

HIGH POSITION
Honor

Bright virtue shines abroad,
Granting endless longevity.
The seven stars of the Big Dipper
Protect and defend me.
I will gain a position of rank and wealth;
If not now, in posterity.

YAN: Above and below are both yang; within and without reflect one another. This is not a time for ordinary pursuits. Now is the time for you to rise to the heights of your sovereignty.

JIE: "Bright virtue shines abroad" means that your powers are in the ascendancy. "The seven stars of the Big Dipper/Protect and defend me" reveals that all obstructions have been cleared away. The Dipper is particularly associated with the passage of time. The time will be right for your action. Now your sovereign strength can be made manifest.

TIME FOR PRAYER
Averting Curses

You keep seeing phantasms
And want to enlist spiritualists.
You'll pray for good fortune,
To avert the disaster you think threatens.
To some extent, you'll find peace;
And a measure of God's power.

YAN: You've seen something that upsets you. There will be trouble at first, but all will turn out as you wish. Also, using dark forces, or spiritual powers, to counteract the bright forces, or events of this world, is something like encountering strange visions when you meditate—you should first look for the disturbance within yourself. Once you have found the solution, you'll see where true spiritual power resides.

JIE: The first line of the poem reveals that your perverse heart has given rise to doubts within. There is discord in the family or hereditary ill-will that you feel powerless to heal. If you confess all, you will, in articulating the problem, certainly be protected.

320

LATE ACHIEVEMENT
Awaiting the Time

Carrying seeds and bending to plow—
The fourth month is a time of scurrying eagerness.
It is hard work to accord with the season,
But the millet grows, row upon row.

YAN: With yang in the top line and yin in the second, all is in its proper position. The sowing of seeds in the proper season leads to great benefits. The fourth month is a time of growing yang, with sprouts appearing in the field.

JIE: With labor at the proper time, great results can be expected. This is a sign that all will proceed smoothly, but you must work in order to reap the harvest.

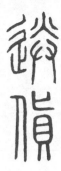

321

DELIVERING MERCHANDISE
Initial Auspiciousness

A guest comes from the south,
Leaving something good for me.
Precious goods, valuable baubles,
Golden bowls, jade cups ...

YAN: Yin powers occupy the center and there is a response from outside. The yang powers are friends coming from afar. South is the direction of yang, so the guest will arrive from the south. The line "Precious goods and valuable baubles" presages wealth, but the fact that some are bowls and cups might indicate a banquet with friends.

JIE: The line "a guest comes from the south" refers to strength responding to weakness. "Golden bowls, jade cups" means that you will be accorded respect. There is great auspiciousness for the one who has thrown this trigram, especially in relation to wealth and sexual partners.

117

322

NO DIFFICULTIES
Peaceful Farming

The land is at peace;
There are no difficulties.
Now is the time for you to sow;
Nothing will impede your going and return.

YAN: In this trigram, there is nothing blocking the top line; thus it is a time for planting seeds and beginning new enterprises.

JIE: "The land is at peace" indicates that your weaknesses have been placed into their appropriate and subordinate positions. "There are no difficulties" means that you are not doubtful or afraid. When the higher and lower aspects of your nature do not combat one another, how could anything go wrong? Everything is auspicious; there will be nothing to block you in your advance or retreat.

RESPECTFUL ACCORD
Harmony

When the one above is square-dealing and
* straightforward,*
Lesser people attend to their tasks.
When there is concord in the family,
Younger and older all work together.
If nothing in your nature opposes your will,
You will achieve whatever you seek.

YAN: It is a time for submissively joining with others, for group action. If you are in a position of authority, you should move only with the support of those below you.

JIE: With the unbending yang in the top position, it is appropriate that you be straightforward and fair—with yourself and with others.

KASHIWA: In all of the three contracts portrayed here—between ruler and the ruled, between family members, and between the various aspects of the self—harmony is important. Once this harmony is achieved, everything can be accomplished.

324

REBELLION
Perversity

The lower does not follow the higher;
The inner does not regulate the outer.
Above and below infringe upon one another;
Thus the ties that bind are sundered.

YAN: Here, dark forces overcome the clear paths of order. This is a sign of perversity and excess. Everything now is inauspicious for you.

JIE: "The lower does not follow the higher": this bespeaks the dominance of yin-like darkness and confusion. "Above and below infringe upon one another" means that personal or external forces overstep their proper positions. When the proper relationships are upset, success is impossible. You may be unwittingly working against yourself.

330

SERVING THE RULER
Joining in Virtue

An enlightened lord is above;
Below there is no hidden evil.
At morning audience, all stand in awe;
With great illumination he passes out promotions.

YAN: With an enlightened lord above and worthy officials below, there are no hidden dangers and all is in order. This trigram is greatly auspicious.

JIE: "At morning audience, all stand in awe" means that there will not be great change. You have reached the height of goodness and all is auspicious. You should be conservative now and not make major changes. If you have asked for rain or other blessings, you will be disappointed.

FRESH OLD AGE
Hidden Powers

The four White-Haired Ones of Mount Shang
Nourished their natures, practiced the Dao.
By breathing the pure air of dawn,
One can achieve agelessness.

YAN: Even though this trigram is entirely yang, the lower line is most active. It betokens a pure nature that can and should be nurtured.

JIE: "The four White-haired Ones of Mount Shang" went into seclusion rather than serve an unjust ruler. This line represents hidden brilliance. "Breathing the pure air of dawn" is a good sign for carefree travel and living life as one wishes. Those who cast this trigram should nurture their excellent qualities in solitude. It is not now appropriate to draw close to or make requests of others.

KASHIWA: Age is largely a state of mind. If they maintain a vivacious spirit, like the fresh air of a new-born day, even the chronologically old are not aged.

332

THE INDOMITABLE
Agreement

Two people of the same heart;
In all things like hand in glove.
Together, they make a kingdom—
Complementing one another's strengths.

YAN: Gains come from relationships with others; losses arise from the self.

JIE: "Two people of the same heart" betokens a doubling of your strength. Your weaknesses have been properly subordinated and will not harm or hinder you. "Complementing one another's strengths" means a sturdy defense against outside evils. In this trigram, the two yang lines above one yin line do not conflict. If you have inquired concerning a relationship with another person, there is nothing inauspicious. You should not second-guess or be suspicious of others. The present time is especially good for business ventures. Do not listen to slanderous words spoken of your associates. Learn to trust others. Allow them to befriend and aid you.

FULLNESS OF STRENGTH
Tuned Muscles

At the height of your flourishing strength,
You are both prosperous and robust.
Use this opportunity to establish merit
And nothing will ever oppose you.

YAN: All three lines of this trigram are greater yang. This is the apex of your powers. It would be most prudent for you now to establish merit by using your advantages to aid others, for it will not be long before you reach the declining phase of your present cycle. If in all things you act with uprightness and without selfishness, avoiding all evil, then there is continued auspiciousness in store for you.

JIE: For those who throw this trigram it is now time to put your strengths into play. Remember that reaching the apex means that diminution is not far away.

334

THE RAVISHING BEAUTY
Apportioned Yin

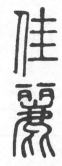

Slate-blue shutters on a purple chamber;
A beauteous concubine resides within.
Her perfect features emit a radiance;
Just as a splendid orchid puts forth perfume.

YAN: Yin forces are in the ascendant here: a woman will manage the affair about which you have inquired. This is because greater yin resides in the bottom line, corresponding above with the greater yang of the second or "humanity" line and the first or "heaven" line. Her strength and virtue emanate like the scent of the orchid.

KASHIWA: In Daoist meditation, the purple chamber often refers to the heart and mind. Here, as elsewhere in the Spirit Tokens, it is not always necessary to look for a person to correspond to each figure in the poem. The beauteous concubine might stand for your own moral purpose.

340

RECEIVING
Long-Term Fortune

Han Lu chases the rabbit;
The flying falcon grasps a pheasant.
No matter what, you will receive it—
At least enough to fill your needs.

YAN: With three yang on top, inner and outer correspond. This is a sign of easy progress and cooperation.

HE: Sometimes things seem to come your way even when you do not seek them. Watch that this easy progress does not result in a lessening of your will to achieve.

341

ACHIEVEMENT
Rising Tides

When lord and minister exchange places,
Great benefit is ensured.
The post rider carries a letter—
Someone will achieve self-satisfaction.

YAN: This is propitious for change and movement. What you have put forward will proceed beneficially. The enterprise you have initiated will receive aid from someone. It will be difficult at first, but harmonious later.

HE: If you now occupy a position, it is time to find a temporary replacement.

JIE: The situation now is exactly the opposite of that in 143. Consult that trigram as well. If your self-satisfaction leads to selfishness, however, there will be great unhappiness.

DELAYED BY DOUBT
Confusion

In your mind you glimpse it,
But doubt it can be done.
Unsure whether to advance or withdraw,
You don't know the next step.

YAN: If you are doubtful, you cannot be single-minded. If you are not singleminded, you won't achieve anything. The massed yin in the lower lines represents psychic blockages which give rise to self-doubt. If you develop your confidence, there will be achievement.

JIE: It may be that you are retarded in your actions by a lesser person who is causing your self-doubts. At any rate, you are still confused about what you ask and there will be no resolution.

343

EVIL DISSOLVES
Bright Reflections

The sun issues from the eastern quadrant,
Blazing, glowing, bright.
Although there are miasmal vapors,
They will be burned away.
The wise dispel the dark around them.
Misfortune and worry are resolved.

YAN: Things may seem strange at first. Don't worry. You have the resources to carry it through.

JIE: Distortion is at its height, but will soon evaporate. Even though you must strive mightily at first, you will succeed. There is danger, but no disaster. All dark affairs are not beneficial.

KASHIWA: "Dark affairs" in the above commentary refers to all manner of secret doings. Now is the time to be open in your actions.

344

THE JUST ONE ABOVE
Brightness

Above there is a worthy ruler,
Below a toadying official.
The sun and moon shine down
But not to the dirt below.

YAN: Although the sun and moon are both bright, they cannot illumine everything, especially not the darkness found in the hearts of people.

HE: There is much deceit operating now, and blockages that have yet to clear away. It is not a good time to act on your impulses, no matter how right they may seem in themselves.

JIE: The various obstructions have not all been cleared; this is not the time to exert your will. Only if you are asking about marriage is this truly a good omen. For all else, there is an equal mixture of good and bad.

Spirit Tokens
of the
Ling Qi Jing

Trigrams
400–444

400

EXPIRATION
Nothingness

Humans are born and die;
They arise again as shades.
The seasons are fixed;
Heat and cold follow one another.
Signs are now unclear—
Forms take shape, but in blackness.

YAN: This is the end of the process described in tri-grams 100, 200, and 300. To view the whole cycle, consult these as well. At the end of a cycle, we are cut off from the sources of creation. With death, yin and yang forces disengage.

HE: Some say that late in life we are beset by myriad "demons." Submission to this interpretation of the life process is the cause of much misfortune.

JIE: At the end of the cycle, everything is dark and hidden. The forms that will give birth to a new cycle begin to take shape, but may not be fully seen.

401

ROBBERS
Bound and Gagged

Robbers are those who wish
To make all treasures their own;
People might fathom their greed,
But demons bind their wrists.

YAN: Now petty people deck themselves out in the gear of the wise, and people struggle with demons.

HE: Find quick relief from these misfortunes. Also, be cautious in what you say now.

JIE: Robbers and riches are equally detestable for what they do to people. It seems that only evil accomplishes things now, but do not let the demons control your actions.

402

LOSS OF REGULATION
Defeat and Blame

By breaking laws and going against reason,
Yin and yang harm one another.
Now Bright Heaven will not help—
We receive only its approbation.

YAN: All matters that follow the eternal principles will go well; those that do not bring disaster.

JIE: Although heaven's laws may be transgressed for a time, the resulting penalties are heavy.

KASHIWA: However you may construe them for the present situation, yin and yang are meant to work in harmony. Now they harm one another instead. The fault lies within you. Search it out.

403

TRAITORS
Suppressing Wisdom

When the crooked enter, the straightforward retire;
There is no way they will stick to the job.
For now the wise hide away;
The sages withdraw with a sigh.

YAN: When the honest are chosen to rule, the people submit. When the dishonest rule, the people will eventually rebel.

HE: Nothing goes smoothly now. Righteous words are not followed. It is best to withdraw and preserve your honesty.

KASHIWA: The political and social implications of this trigram are obvious, but it might also apply to purely personal matters. You may be repressing your better instincts.

404

THE TONGUES
Deteriorating Fortunes

The eastern neighbor takes a wife;
The western neighbor entertains guests.
The bound pig squeals and snorts;
The beaten dog yowls and howls.
Be prepared for changing fortunes.
Do not let them turn to tragedy.

YAN: This matter begins with your meeting people and events that may lead to unexpected good fortune in your home.

HE: There is potential conflict here, with the eastern neighbor celebrating a wedding while the western neighbor invites guests. On both sides there is the sound of pigs being prepared for a feast, and dogs tied up for the guests' arrival. There is strife and bragging.

JIE: There are signs that strife is imminent. If you do nothing to avert it, there will be trouble. Guard against greed now.

410

CLEANSING SHAME
Bearing Other's Ascent

The wife, bearing food, enters the fields;
She doesn't see her husband plowing.
As she seeks her husband, a crow shamelessly
  filches his sandwich meat.
With bent bow he fires at it;
The arrow strikes its left wing.

YAN: The yang energy in the middle position is isolated and weak, covered by yin. There is harm in this situation. But despite its weakness, this is a growing yang so it will eventually strengthen, wiping out the shame of loss.

HE: In your dealings with someone there is cause for regret. This is a sign of impending trouble.

JIE: Your strength is little and the task is great. The numerous obstructions you now face will eventually be overcome and you will grow in the process.

ORPHANED AND POOR
Meeting Hardship

Pushed from the warm into the cold,
Coat thin, clothes unlined,
I leave my loving mother and go
Into this flawed and sorrowful world.

YAN: The single yang lines covered by yin betoken leaving the place or people one loves and meeting hard companions. This is an inauspicious omen. Since this is a sign of parting, it is best you cling to the old and true. In the second month you will receive, but all other months are bare.

HE: It is best that you protect what you have now. The new season will bring a change.

JIE: Like an orphan, you lack support now.

A SUBMERGED DRAGON
Awaiting the Right Moment

Shun bent low to cultivate his fields,
Down to the edge of Mount Experience.
The earth was fruitful, the harvest great—
He measured it in the thousands of bushels.

YAN: One labours in obscurity toward the day of rich harvests, just as the ancient sage-king, Shun, when unjustly driven out by his parents, cultivated his fields near the Mountain of Experience. By concealing and protecting yourself now, you can cultivate your inner resources. Then there will be nothing, great or small, that cannot be achieved through your efforts.

JIE: There is a concentration of yin in the upper line of this trigram that seems to cover all, vouchsafing nothing. But, in the fullness of your virtue, there will be a response from below. When the time comes, there will be nothing opposing you.

413

AN INCREASE IN FRIENDSHIP
Responding to the Omen

A guest, a veritable princess,
Comes to knock on my door.
She speaks of my Good Fortune.
If I go, I may expect her grace.

YAN: Only when someone (or something) calls will it be appropriate for you to proceed. If someone has summoned and you have not responded, it is inauspicious. Since the inside responds to the outside, the answer is not within. The fulfillment of your will is in departing, in seeking what is outside of you.

JIE: "A veritable princess knocks on the door" means that there is a response to your situation from without. "If I go, I may expect her grace" means that there is aid to be sought. The "princess" is any person of power and influence. The middle line is lesser yang, which does not struggle, but aids; thus there is good fortune in going. That which have asked should proceed as you wish. There will be aid from someone with power.

414

LONGSTANDING ENMITIES
Much Hardship

Promises broken, we live apart,
Again and again cursing one another.
Nothing here is advantageous,
Nothing we try succeeds.

YAN: Nothing will go as you wish. In response, you feel fearful, like the single yang line in the middle which seems to have no support. But despite repeated setbacks, if you hide away during this time of difficulty, you will find wholeness. If this is an old question, now is not the time. If it is a new one, all is inauspicious, ask again later.

JIE: If you have not kept your promises, what can you expect from others? Weak and alone, you can begin nothing new now.

KASHIWA: Rather than worrying, you should dispassionately examine the processes that brought you to ask this question. Think about rebuilding your support systems.

PLAYING HOST TO BRIGANDS
Harmful Processes

Drunk on liquor they began to argue—
Now a knife and a staff are raised in anger.
The host trembles in fear;
Through restraining himself, he averts a melee.

YAN: You are in a position of powerlessness, buried under massed yin forces. "Guests," or outside influences, have lost decorum and now drunkenly brawl. Only because the host humbles himself and suppresses his frightened response is the situation restored to normal. This trigram betokens great enmities. Meeting with such a "guest" now is the worst of calamities.

HE: At first there will be bitter words, but finally no real worries.

JIE: As long as you don't try to act, but merely protect yourself right now, everything will be just fine.

421

SPIRITUAL AID
Saved from the Depths

Four ghosts, two shamans
Face one another and bow.
Heavenly spirits descend below
To release those bound in hell.
Misfortune thus calls forth healing.
You will receive heavenly blessing.

YAN: All things are now liberated. The single yang in the third line is able to eradicate illness and dispel calamity, like shamans descending into hell to rescue the souls bound there. Everything is at first highly inauspicious, but all will end well.

JIE: "Four ghosts and two shamans" means that yin forces are ascendant. The fact that heavenly spirits bring blessings means that once the yin has reached its apogee, good things follow. The "depths of negativity" is precisely the time when one should take hope, since greatness follows.

EXORCISM
Praying for Good Fortune

A tomb mound, a high hill—
Ghosts and spirits roam here.
Pray for their quick release
And you may be without worry.

YAN: The way of ghosts and spirits is now evident. Pray and make offerings and you will be without worry.

HE: There are spiritual forces you have not employed. Employ them and all will go well. Or, if you notice weird apparitions, you should propitiate them.

JIE: "A tomb mound, a high hill" means that the influences of the dead are strong. Immediately come to terms with them, and these forces will work for you rather than against you. Only by accepting the hidden energies at work here will you be able to avoid disaster. You should not contend, but should be yielding in your rectitude.

423

THE LAST LAUGH
Release

The metal spirit wishes to rise.
You must depend on someone stronger.
Block it with your left hand,
Then you will gain a benefactor.

YAN: Metal belongs to the west and is the position of lesser yin. It controls weapons and killing. The left is the yang side. This means that when yin forces begin to rise, the truly great person counters with an appropriate response. This trigram indicates that there is something to worry about, but it will not become a severe disorder if you act properly.

JIE: You should find the appropriate person to aid you in that which you have inquired about. At first you need to be cautious; then you will be content.

424

PRAYING FOR BENEFIT
Initial Auspiciousness

Offerings made in the ancestral temple
Dissolve evil forces.
Blessing comes to fill your gate;
Disorder flees five thousand miles.

YAN: You should ask your forebears for their blessings with regard to the matter you have inquired about.

JIE: "Offerings made in the ancestral temple" means you should rely on spiritual aid and accept it with reverence. One who is reverent and obedient to the traditions of the ancestors will not lose decorum and will reap rewards. Those who do not learn the lessons of history will have cause for regret.

430

AVOIDING CONTRARINESS
Know When to Stop

Ahead there are brigands;
Behind, you see no travellers.
For safe travel, stop now—
It will save your life.

YAN: The three yang rest below, while the massed yin in the top line are like the "bandits ahead". While there is no felicity here, at least you can preserve yourself.

HE: Some might argue that it would be best to return to a town, and the safety others provide, but it is prudent just to stop where you are for a while.

JIE: If you see the troubles ahead and modify your expectations, there will be no disaster.

431

FOLLOW YOUR HEART
Walking Towards Greatness

Mysterious clouds cover you above,
Below there are no deceivers.
Everything flows along—
All returns to its true state.

YAN: Everything goes as you wish. Others will aid you in this matter. The yin forces occupy the top line and are properly honored by the yang forces below.

HE: This trigram indicates that you should make your move in the autumn.

JIE: Your powers are at their height and no one works against you. Everything will proceed smoothly.

432

RETRIEVING THE LOST
The Victorious and Strong

Having taken away my precious gems,
Taken them from heaven's crossroads,
Unexpectedly, the thief
Hid them in his own house.
I depend on the Dusky Bird
Who drives on before me.
The winds are stilled, the waves quieted;
I return the gems to my dwelling.

YAN: At first, you will be thwarted, but all will end as you wish. Someone will bring you something. While thieves surround you, stealing your treasures, you are able to divine their secret plots, just like the mythical Dusky Bird was said to drive off evil fowl.

JIE: The yin forces are at their apex in the top line and growing stronger in the bottom line, but the full yang in the middle is able to counteract them. This is a sign that your own powers are more than sufficient for the task ahead. If you seek help from someone, you will also garner good results.

433

RESCUE
Receiving Succor

The Director of Destinies descends
To examine the books of life.
Your span of life is not up,
But you are untimely afflicted and withering.
He orders Bian Que to aid you;
Has him open his jewelled flask
And give one medicinal pill.
So your life is restored.

YAN: Although your forces are in their proper positions, there is blockage. If you are aware of the difficulties ahead, you will not be destroyed by calamity. Instead, you will gain positive benefits from adversity. An excellent doctor like Bian Que can be expected to aid you.

HE: In a bureaucracy, documents flutter back and forth and only at last are put in order. Those who hold our "books of life" are like this. Sometimes the evil that befalls us is simply a mistake. Know this and it will not be so hard to bear.

434

THE GREAT CONDUIT
Emerging

Vast, the Crossroads of Heaven
Reaches in all directions, up and down.
We travel along it,
Riding clouds, reining dragons.

YAN: The regal in spirit gain command of the forces around them. The base in spirit will not achieve victory, but in fact may bring disaster upon themselves. Also, if you aid the cause of enlightenment, there is no blame, and all that you seek will be as you wish.

HE: Your forces will be nourished. You will gradually achieve greatness. But remember, this is not a sign to be taken lightly.

JIE: One who draws this trigram can rectify the nation and bring peace to the people. If you eradicate cruelty and ruthlessness, there is nothing you cannot achieve.

440

ENTANGLEMENTS
A Time for Haste

Hanging dangerously, as if bound;
Help fails to arrive.
The state of Lu looked to Gaozi.
You should not imitate them.

YAN: When your yang powers are completely dissipated, yin powers pour fully into the breach. This is a sign of defeat and confusion, but ultimate good fortune if you heed the lesson here: The kingdom of Lu made an alliance with Qi, but Gaozi of that state ultimately destroyed them. Do not look to others to save you. You must now move swiftly in all matters. If you hesitate, you will find no harmony.

JIE: In this trigram the yin forces begin to move upwards and disaster must come. If you look to others for help, you will be in particularly tight straits.

44I

SUNK IN THE HAZE
Indistinct Images

Constantly gazing about,
Now you're without energy.
You raise your face to call on heaven;
Then lower your head to bury it in your breast.
You seek without finding;
Look without seeing.

YAN: There is a single yang below, buried in the earth. The massed yin forces obscure it, so that it lowers its head, falling prostrate on the ground. This trigram is very inauspicious.

HE: The time is inappropriate for all you have asked—you can only sigh. You must learn to nurture good fortune to drive off the evil influences.

KASHIWA: You are looking in the wrong direction. You can "nurture good fortune" by discerning in the haze that surrounds you now not confirmation of your present confusion, but the first signs of what is to come.

442

EXTENDED YIN
Expiring Within

Layered yin rests above;
Demon breaths float about.
When there is water in the courtyard,
You can leave the house by boat.

YAN: This trigram is totally yin. Inner and outer do not correspond to one another. The calamities brought about by demons and officials all belong to the yin powers. This is a sign of evil and deterioration in all matters.

JIE: "Water in the courtyard" indicates that you may be drowning in your problems. Whoever obtains this trigram should guard against yin types: thieves, robbers, slanderers, and secret plotters. More importantly, they should guard against inner darkness.

KASHIWA: No matter how dark things seem, something can be gained from the situation.

443

AVOIDING THE WORLD
Severe Trouble

Hemmed in by evil and misfortune,
You shut the door and sit alone.
Friends and associates scatter;
There is no one from whom to borrow a light.

YAN: Your yang powers have lost their place. There is no aid for you. The "light" here is the needed yang. Whatever aid others might have brought you is now blocked.

JIE: You are blinding yourself to the ominous forces gathering around you. This is no way to deal with problems! Whoever draws this trigram will probably suffer what they call "misfortune," but it is all the result of ignorance.

444

MYRIAD MISFORTUNES
Falling from Grace

Evil arrives with sudden violence;
Nothing at all goes smoothly.
Illness after sickness, all in a series;
When you move — you're in head over heels.

YAN: All three positions are yin: there must be misfortune. Going, staying, speaking, keeping silence, nothing is propitious.

HE: Nothing goes smoothly. Take care and avoid evil. Things will soon level out. Flowers are born from frost-filled skies, but now smoke-flowers fill your eyes. Do not exhaust your capabilities— human affairs are now topsy-turvy. Accept it.

JIE: Everything you try to do now will meet with blockage. You can only wait until the troubles dissolve.

靈樞經

ABOUT THE AUTHOR

Ivan Kashiwa wishes to remain anonymous. This much can be told: Some twenty years ago, Kashiwa, one of a handful of researchers into the religion of Daoism at that time, was at a crossroads in his life. The reopening of China to the outside world put significant pressure on him to give up his "fruitless" scholarly work and enter a career in business. Just then, Kashiwa came upon a book of photolithographic reproductions of Dunhuang manuscripts in a Japanese library basement—a book cache almost as dusty as the desert grotto where Stein and Pelliot intially encountered the texts. The book fell open to the *Ling Qi Jing*. Kashiwa decided to take his dilemma to the text. The trigram he cast with the Japanese coins in his pocket that day was Trigram ooo. After pondering it, he returned to his studies, and today teaches and lectures on Daoism.

Why is Kashiwa reluctant to tell you more about himself? The answer is simple. The authors of the *Ling Qi Jing* and its commentaries—who made this book a living thing— have never chosen to use its popularity to enhance their own. Kashiwa agrees with them. And so does the *Ling Qi Jing*.

The "weathermark" identifies this book as a production of Weatherhill, Inc., publishers of fine books on Asia and the Pacific. Editorial supervision, book and cover design: David S. Noble. Production supervision: Bill Rose. Printed and bound by Daamen, Inc. The typeface used is Columbus.